CAN I
Lose My
SALVATION?

R.C. SPROUL

IR *Reformation Trust*   A DIVISION OF LIGONIER MINISTRIES, ORLANDO, FL

Can I Lose My Salvation?

© 2015 by R.C. Sproul

Published by Reformation Trust Publishing
a division of Ligonier Ministries
421 Ligonier Court, Sanford, FL 32771
Ligonier.org   ReformationTrust.com

Printed in North Mankato, MN
Corporate Graphics
June 2016
First edition, second printing

Cover design: Gearbox Studios
Interior design and typeset: Katherine Lloyd, The DESK

All Scripture quotations are from *The Holy Bible, English Standard Version*, copyright © 2001 by Crossway Bibles, a division of Good News Publishers. Used by permission. All rights reserved.

Library of Congress Cataloging-in-Publication Data

Sproul, R. C. (Robert Charles), 1939-
 Can I lose my salvation? / by R.C. Sproul. -- First edition.
   pages cm. -- (Crucial questions series ; No. 22)
 ISBN 978-1-56769-499-4
1. Assurance (Theology) 2. Salvation--Christianity. I. Title.
 BT785.S675 2015
 234--dc23
                              2015018384

Contents

Chapter One

STONES OF
REMEMBRANCE

Soon after I became a Christian in college, a friend of mine took me to meet an elderly lady who lived alone in a small trailer. This woman was one of the most radiant Christian women I have ever met. She was an authentic prayer warrior; she would pray eight hours every day for all kinds of concerns. My friend explained to this lady that I had just recently become a Christian. Delighted, she looked at me and said, "Young man, what you need to do is drive a spiritual stake in the ground right now." I had no idea what she was talking about, but she explained to me that I needed to make sure that my conversion was forever. I was to remember this time in my life, the moment of my conversion, so that when I would come to struggles in the future, I would look back to that moment.

Her advice was reminiscent of an event in the book of Joshua, which tells the story of the Israelites' entering the Promised Land. The Israelites had gone through the exodus, the crossing of the Red Sea, and the forty years of wandering in the wilderness. Now, finally, they were preparing to enter Canaan. But this final leg of the journey wouldn't be easy, either.

Between them and the Promised Land was the Jordan River. It was at flood stage; it had overflowed its banks and was about a mile wide. And of course, on the other side were the Canaanites, who had heard of Israel's approach and were preparing to meet them.

As the people of Israel stood by the river, God gave Joshua their marching orders: the priests were to advance to the water carrying the ark of the covenant. As they stepped into the water, the river rolled back twenty miles and the riverbed was dry. And so this whole body of people crossed over the Jordan into the Promised Land.

Then Joshua gave the people an assignment:

When all the nation had finished passing over the Jordan, the LORD said to Joshua, "Take twelve men from the people, from each tribe a man, and command them, saying, 'Take twelve stones from here out of the midst of the Jordan, from the very place where the priests' feet stood firmly, and bring them over with you and lay them down in the place where you lodge tonight.'" Then Joshua called the twelve men from the people of Israel, whom he had appointed, a man from each tribe. And Joshua said to them, "Pass on before the ark of the LORD your God into the midst of the Jordan, and take up each of you a stone upon his shoulder, according to the number of the tribes of the people of Israel, that this may be a sign among you. When your children ask in time to come, 'What do those stones mean to you?' then you shall tell them that the waters of the Jordan were cut off before the ark of the covenant of the LORD. When it passed over the Jordan, the waters of the Jordan were cut off. So these stones shall be to the people of Israel a memorial forever." (Josh. 4:1–7)

The people were to put a pillar of twelve stones in the middle of this riverbed as a memorial to this event. Then, representatives from each tribe were each to take a stone from the riverbed and set up a memorial at Gilgal, where they were staying that night.

There are examples of this kind of memorial-making throughout the Old Testament. Noah built an altar upon being rescued from the ravages of the flood (Gen. 8:20–22). Jacob set up a memorial after his vision of the ladder reaching to heaven (Gen. 28:10–22). David built an altar at the spot where a plague from the Lord stopped (1 Sam. 24). These monuments marked decisive moments in history for all future generations so that when the people of Israel were afraid and needed consolation, they could look and see this reminder that God was with them. He had brought them thus far and He had promised to take them the rest of the way. In other words, these memorials were to be visible reminders for the people in the midst of their struggle, in the midst of their doubts, in the midst of their fears, to look to the God who had delivered them in the first place.

As my friend impressed upon me, we need this kind of reminder in an uncertain world. As we struggle through the Christian life, we sometimes wrestle with our security in Christ. We want to be safe, to feel secure, and we need assurance that our security will last. The key question here is, "Can a person who is truly and soundly converted to Christ lose his or her salvation?" Or, more personally, "Can *I* lose my salvation?" This gets at the issue of the doctrine of eternal security, also known as the perseverance of the saints, which is the *P* in the famous Calvinist acronym *TULIP*.

This being such a crucial issue for believers, it has sparked great controversy through the history of the church, leading to a variety of answers to the question. During the sixteenth century, the Roman Catholic Church disputed with the Reformers because the Reformers said that a person can be justified by faith alone, and upon their justification, they can have an assurance of their present state of salvation. But the Reformers made a distinction between *assurance of salvation*—that is, certainty that one is currently saved, with no comment on whether one will remain saved—and *perseverance of the saints*—certainty that one will continue to be saved into the eternal future. Rome denies the doctrine of eternal security and even denies the doctrine of the assurance of salvation except for a special, elite group of saints such as the Virgin Mary or

Francis of Assisi. Because Rome has always taught that one can commit a mortal sin and thus lose salvific grace, they opposed the Reformation concept of perseverance or eternal security.

Within the Reformation itself, there was a dispute between the Lutherans and the Reformed because many Lutheran theologians took the position that a person can have a present assurance of salvation, but that saving faith can be lost, and with it, one's justification. In the later development of the Reformed churches, there was a fierce debate in the Netherlands. A group called the Remonstrants modified Dutch Calvinism and argued against the perseverance of the saints, taking the position that salvation can be lost.

In the Bible itself, there are many passages that strongly suggest that people can indeed lose their salvation (e.g., Heb. 6:4–6; 2 Peter 2:20–22). And yet, on the other side, there are also many passages that seem to be promises that God will preserve His people to the end. In the latter category, for instance, there is Paul's statement that "he who began a good work in you will bring it to completion at the day of Jesus Christ" (Phil. 1:6). Scripture has a unified message, but it's difficult at times to reconcile these two sets of teachings. And in the final analysis, it is through looking at Scripture that the question should be resolved.

In the ancient church, the Latin phrase that was used in connection with this debate was *militia christianae*. This phrase has to do with the ongoing struggle of the Christian life. I think that's where we live—not in the abstract environment of philosophical or theological concepts, but in the midst of a real sense of struggle in our daily lives as Christians. The idea of *militia christianae* points to the struggle of the Christian life, the struggle of the Christian who is called to endure in the faith.

We remember Jesus' statement that "the one who endures to the end will be saved" (Matt. 24:13). We think also of when Jesus said, "No one who puts his hand to the plow and looks back is fit for the kingdom of God" (Luke 9:62). Jesus warns those who have come out of false beliefs and embraced the faith not to look back.

Clearly, there are those who seem to make a credible profession of faith and then later repudiate that profession of faith. I think that anyone who has been a Christian for more than a year knows people like that, people who, to all outward appearances, seem to have been dedicated to Christianity and then later left the faith or left the church.

And so we have to ask the question: How is that possible, if we are to maintain the idea that one who was once in grace will remain in grace?

This question can get very personal, as well. It's not just theoretical. As we experience the ups and downs of life, those changes that are part of the impermanency of our daily experience, we are tempted to raise the ultimate question: If I'm presently in a state of faith, if I'm presently embracing Christ, will that change? Will the status that I enjoy in the presence of God change? Can I lose my salvation?

Chapter Two

THOSE WHO FALL AWAY

There are perhaps few things as complicated as the golf swing. There are a hundred things to remember, and keeping track of every little thing can feel overwhelming. Picking up the game can take hours upon hours of practice, and it seems that it can never truly be mastered.

Over the course of my playing career, there have been many times when I've learned a *swing key*—a drill, position, or something else to focus on—that I thought would transform my game. I would be so excited to go out on the golf course and try this key, and I would be thrilled as the key would work in an amazingly productive manner, helping me shoot a great round of golf.

One day, after using a particular swing key, I thought I had it all figured out. But my golf pro warned me that there is a junior-grade deity who hangs around golf courses waiting for golfers to think they've got it figured out. Then he takes it all away.

The phenomenon of the transient usefulness of swing keys once led me to accept the existence of what I call "WOOD keys," meaning "works only one day." I've had lots of WOOD keys. I repeat the exact same technique that I used the first time, but on the second day, nothing seems to be working right. I've certainly relied on a few of those WOOD keys, and my golf game has advanced one day, only to fall again the next day.

The Bible speaks about this dynamic in the life of some professing believers. What we're describing here theologically is called *apostasy*, a term based on a Greek word meaning "to stand away from." To fall into apostasy means to reach a position but then to abandon it. So, when we talk about those who have become apostate or who have committed apostasy, we're talking about those who have fallen from the faith or at least have fallen from their first profession of faith. This is the exact topic we're discussing when we ask questions about the doctrine of eternal security or the perseverance of the saints. We're asking: Is it possible for a Christian who's truly regenerated, who truly believes in Christ, to apostatize?

There are many texts in the New Testament that warn about this presumed possibility. Paul admonishes the Corinthians, "Therefore, let him who thinks he stands take heed lest he fall" (1 Cor. 10:14). Is Paul merely rebuking a kind of arrogance whereby a person has a false assurance of his standing, or is he warning against ever coming to the conclusion that you are in a state of grace that cannot be lost? Those who argue against the doctrine of eternal security say Paul was here clearly denying such a teaching and warning against it. Since it hardly seems likely that Paul would warn against the possibility of such a fall if indeed such a fall were manifestly impossible, they interpret this verse to be a denial of the possibility of eternal security.

Another verse that is sometimes regarded as evidence against the guaranteed perseverance of the saints appears in Paul's first letter to Timothy. Near the end of his life and ministry, Paul urges his protégé to fight the good fight of faith:

This charge I entrust to you, Timothy, my child, in accordance with the prophecies previously made about you, that by them you may wage the good warfare, holding faith and a good conscience. By rejecting this, some have made shipwreck of their faith, among whom are Hymenaeus and Alexander, whom I have handed over to Satan that they may learn not to blaspheme. (1 Tim. 1:18–20)

Here, Paul gives instructions and admonitions that are related to the battle or the good fight of the faith, the ongoing struggle of the Christian life. He warns Timothy to keep the faith and a good conscience and to be reminded of those who didn't. He also speaks of particular individuals, Hymenaeus and Alexander, who, first of all, made shipwreck of their faith; and, second of all, were actually excommunicated by the Apostle (this is what is meant by having "handed [them] over to Satan that they may learn not to blaspheme"). So, here we have not just an abstract warning but a specific, personal warning coupled with concrete examples of people who apparently have experienced a grievous fall away from the purity of their Christian faith.

Elsewhere, Paul himself speaks of pummeling his body

to subdue it and of being involved in the discipline of the things of God lest, he says, "I myself should be disqualified" (1 Cor. 9:27). Paul thus sets before the reader, at least hypothetically, the possibility that he, even as the Apostle to the Gentiles, might become disqualified. This wording is similar to that in Jesus' warnings in the Sermon on the Mount that many would come to him on the last day, saying, "Lord, Lord, did we not prophesy in your name, and cast out demons in your name, and do many mighty works in your name?" and He will say, "I never knew you; depart from me, you workers of lawlessness" (Matt. 7:22–23).

Of course, the strongest warning against apostasy in all of Scripture is found in Hebrews 6, which is so important to this discussion that it receives its own treatment in chapter four of this book.

It is perfectly clear from the text of 1 Timothy 1, as well as narrative examples that we find in the Scriptures— for example, the well-known leaders King David and the Apostle Peter—that it is certainly possible for people who profess faith in Jesus Christ to fall in some sense of the word. We noticed in the case of Hymenaeus and Alexander that Paul had excommunicated them for their own instruction that they might learn not to blaspheme. Several questions remain, however, about the nature of the spiritual crises that are recorded for us in Scripture and of the egregious occasions when professing believers fall and fall radically. These questions have to do with whether there are different degrees of falling and whether falling radically means that one has irretrievably lost one's salvation.

The Italian Reformed scholar Girolamo Zanchi once made the distinction between a *serious fall* and a *total fall*. He argued that the Bible is replete with examples of true believers who truly fall away, who fall into gross sin and, on some occasions, protracted periods of impenitence. This is a *serious fall*. An example is David, who remained impenitent regarding his sin with Bathsheba for more than a year before he was brought back to repentance and renewal of his faith. So, the question is not "Do people fall?" They do fall. Each and every Christian is subject to the possibility of a serious fall. But is someone who commits a serious fall eternally lost—making it a *total fall*—or is the fall a temporary condition that will be remedied by his restoration?

Church discipline has the aim of restoring those who have made a profession of faith but then live in great, impenitent sin. In other words, church discipline attempts to keep a serious fall from turning into a total fall. There are stages or steps to church discipline, the final step of which is excommunication. But when a person is excommunicated from fellowship in the church and is considered by the church as being in the same state as an unbeliever, even that is designed to reclaim and to recover that person, to see him restored to fellowship. Similarly, when Paul handed Hymenaeus and Alexander over to Satan, he still held out hope that through such a disciplinary process they would come to their senses and be restored once again to the fellowship of Christ.

While some will return after a serious fall, some will not, because they never actually had faith. They made a false profession of faith; they did not possess what they professed. When the heat comes, such a person will flee from his original profession, resulting in a total fall. In cases like this, the conversion was not genuine in the first place. This is illustrated in Jesus' parable of the sower (Matt. 13:1–9). In that parable, the seed that falls on different kinds of ground—the hard ground of the path, rocky ground, ground covered with thorns, and the good soil. In some cases, the seed germinates initially, but it is withered by the noonday sun or choked by the thorns. As Jesus explains, the parable refers to people and how they receive the Word as it comes to them (vv. 18–23). Some receive the Word and profess faith but do not endure; they fall away.

The Apostle John speaks of those who went out from the midst of the communion of fellowship. He said: "They went out from us, but they were not of us; for if they had been of us, they would have continued with us. But they went out, that it might become plain that they all are not of us" (1 John 2:19). So John, at least in that particular incident, does speak clearly under the inspiration of the Holy Spirit about certain people who departed from the faith, and he says of those people, "they were not of us." At least in this particular case, he is describing the apostasy of people who had made a profession of faith but who were never really converted.

The challenge, then, is to distinguish between a true believer in the midst of a serious fall (who will at some point in the future be restored) and a person who has made a false profession of faith. We cannot read the hearts of others, so we do not know, when we see a person who has made a profession of faith later repudiate that profession, whether the person may yet be a true convert who is only temporarily abandoning his profession and will return to it.

Many of us have known friends or family members who seemed for all outward appearances to have made a genuine profession of faith. We thought their profession was credible. We embraced them as brothers or sisters, only to find out that they later repudiated that faith. What are we to do in a situation like that? I recommend at least two responses: first, pray like crazy, and second, wait. We don't know the final outcome of the situation, but God does, and only God can preserve that soul.

Chapter Three

THE
UNFORGIVABLE SIN

I frequently receive letters from around the world. People write in asking questions—sometimes the questions are more academic, and sometimes they are more personal and practical. Very often, possibly at least once a month, I get a letter from someone who is profoundly concerned that he or she has committed the unforgivable sin spoken of by Jesus. While this is a biblical and theological issue, it's not an abstract one, as these folks are profoundly tormented by that concern. The question of whether or not we can fall out of God's good graces touches us at the core of our faith and our lives.

The warning about the unforgivable sin that comes from Jesus is contained in each of the Synoptic Gospels. When considering this issue, it's important to keep in mind the context, as without the context, we run the risk of misunderstanding what Jesus is referring to. To get a sense of the context, let's look at Matthew's account:

> Then a demon-oppressed man who was blind and mute was brought to him, and he healed him, so that the man spoke and saw. And all the people were amazed, and said, "Can this be the Son of David?" But when the Pharisees heard it, they said, "It is only by Beelzebul, the prince of demons, that this man casts out demons." (Matt. 12:22–24)

The issue of the unforgivable sin arises after Jesus heals a demon-possessed man, which astonished the people who observed the healing and immediately inspired the question, "Can this be the son of David?" which is to say, "Is this the Messiah?"

However, the Pharisees, who were in fierce opposition to

Jesus, suggested an alternative interpretation of the event. They weren't ready to accede that Jesus had performed this miracle by virtue of His being the Messiah; rather, they said He was borrowing power from Satan himself. They said He did these things by the power of the Beelzebul—"lord of the flies," a title for Satan.

Notice that neither side denied the reality of the power that was exhibited on that occasion. The question was the source of that power and the identity of the person who was exercising that power. Let's go on with the text:

> Knowing their thoughts, he said to them, "Every kingdom divided against itself is laid waste, and no city or house divided against itself will stand. And if Satan casts out Satan, he is divided against himself. How then will his kingdom stand? And if I cast out demons by Beelzebul, by whom do your sons cast them out? Therefore they will be your judges. But if it is by the Spirit of God that I cast out demons, then the kingdom of God has come upon you. Or how can someone enter a strong man's house and plunder his goods, unless he first binds the strong man? Then indeed he

may plunder his house. Whoever is not with me is against me, and whoever does not gather with me scatters." (vv. 25–30)

Jesus says, in effect, "This isn't the power of Satan. This is the power of God and, specifically, the power of God the Holy Spirit." This is the context in which the Holy Spirit is brought into the discussion. Then Jesus gives his dreadful warning:

Therefore I tell you, every sin and blasphemy will be forgiven people, but the blasphemy against the Spirit will not be forgiven. And whoever speaks a word against the Son of Man will be forgiven, but whoever speaks against the Holy Spirit will not be forgiven, either in this age or in the age to come. (vv. 31–32)

There's a technical point to be made about calling this sin the "unforgivable sin." What do we mean by *unforgivable*? In the very strictest meaning of the term, it means "unable to be forgiven." But, technically speaking, God has the ability to forgive any sin if He so desires. So, when we call it the "unforgivable sin," we mean by that that it is a sin that will in fact not be forgiven by God, not because God *can't* do it but God *won't* do it. That's the warning that Jesus makes to those who are charging Him with doing His miracles by the power of Satan. He warns them that there is a sin that God will not forgive either in this world or in the world to come.

What is more difficult to understand is that Jesus also says that people can sin against the Son of Man and be forgiven, but they won't be forgiven if they sin against the Holy Spirit. That's hard to conceptualize for the simple reason that we believe in the Trinity—one God in three persons. There's the Father, the Son, and the Holy Spirit, and these three are one God; the "Son of Man" refers to the second person of the Trinity. Why would sinning against the second person of the Trinity be forgivable but a particular sin against the third person not be forgivable?

There is a somewhat simple solution to this dilemma. Notice that Jesus doesn't say that it's *any* sin against the Holy Spirit that is unforgivable. We sin against the Holy Spirit all the time. In fact, every sin that we commit as Christians is an offense to the Spirit of holiness who dwells within us to work for our sanctification. And if every sin against the Holy Spirit were unforgivable, none of us could ever be forgiven. So, Jesus is being very narrow and specific here about a particular kind of sin, one that He defines as blasphemy against the Holy Spirit.

We have to be careful here, because He's also not saying that *any* form of blasphemy that has ever committed is unforgivable. Again, if any blasphemy were unforgivable, we would never be forgiven. Every time we use the Lord's name in vain, it is an act of blasphemy. But the Bible makes it abundantly clear that on His cross, Christ reconciled blasphemers to God. Rather than making a blanket statement about blasphemous words, Jesus is defining a sin here in an extremely specific, particular, narrow sense. Not all blasphemies are unforgivable, not all sins against the Holy Spirit are unforgivable, and not all sins against the Son of Man are unforgivable. So, what is specifically in view here?

This question has been answered in many ways over the course of church history. Some have assumed that the unforgivable sin is murder, because the Old Testament prescribes capital punishment for that crime, but that answer misses the point—murder is not blasphemy. In trying to understand the nature of this grievous sin, we need to start with the fact that it's identified as blasphemy, and blasphemy has to do with words. Under normal circumstances, blasphemy is something that comes from the mouth. It has to do with what we say. We can see this in the verb Jesus uses: he specifies whoever *speaks against* the Holy Spirit. Thus, blasphemy is not a sinful act in general, or even the sinful act of murder, but rather an action of the tongue.

In biblical ethics, there is a great concern for patterns of human speech. We've seen already that in the first petition of the Lord's Prayer, Christ tells us to pray that the name of God may be hallowed, that it may be considered sacred and treated with reverence and with respect; anything less than that is blasphemous. All blasphemy is a serious offense against God, and the frequency with which it is committed in this world in no way diminishes the severity of the wickedness of this act. But in this particular case, we're talking about a certain type of blasphemy and not blasphemy in general.

Jesus is responding to the Pharisees, who have been engaged in consistently fierce opposition to Him. They were the ones who were most knowledgeable in the things of God, in the law of God, in the theology of the Old Testament. If any group of people should have been the first ones to recognize the identity of Christ as the Son of Man and as the promised Messiah, it was the Pharisees. But, instead, they were the ones who most fiercely opposed Him.

At the same time, there is an acute awareness in the New Testament of a profound ignorance that veils the eyes of the Pharisees. We see this at the cross, and then we see it in 1 Corinthians. On the cross, when Jesus prays for the forgiveness of those who had delivered Him for His execution, He says, "Father, forgive them, for they know not what they do" (Luke 23:34). And in 1 Corinthians, Paul writes, "None of the rulers of this age understood this, for if they had, they would not have crucified the Lord of glory" (1:8).

Jesus' response appears to be a warning to the Pharisees that they are coming perilously close to a line past which there will be no hope for them. Before that line is crossed, Jesus can pray for their forgiveness on the basis of their ignorance, but past that point, there is no forgiveness.

During His earthly life, Christ's glory was veiled. But once He was raised by the Holy Spirit and had made Himself known, through the Holy Spirit, as the Son of God, then to say that Christ performed His works through the power of Satan rather than through the power of the Holy Spirit would be going too far.

Thus, someone commits the unforgivable sin when he

knows for certain through the illumination of the Spirit that Christ is the Son of God, but he comes to the conclusion and makes the statement verbally that Christ was demonic. The book of Hebrews summarizes the issue for us:

> For if we go on sinning deliberately after receiving the knowledge of the truth, there no longer remains a sacrifice for sins. . . . How much worse punishment, do you think, will be deserved by the one who has trampled underfoot the Son of God, and has profaned the blood of the covenant by which he was sanctified, and has outraged the Spirit of grace? (Heb. 10:26, 29)

Therefore, the distinction between blaspheming the Holy Spirit and blaspheming against Christ falls away once the person knows who Jesus is.

We know that one of the most important works that is performed by the Holy Spirit in the life of the Christian is to convict us of sin. And the purpose of the Spirit's work of convicting us of sin is to lead us to repentance to the end that we may be forgiven and restored to the fullness of fellowship with God.

To people who fear that they may have committed the unforgivable sin, I often say that had they actually committed it, in all likelihood they would not be disturbed by it. Their hearts would have already become so recalcitrant and hardened that they would not be struggling and wrestling with it. People who commit such sin don't care about it, and the very fact that these people are wrestling with the fear that perhaps they have offended God in this way gives significant evidence to the reality that they are not in such a state.

Chapter Four

IMPOSSIBLE TO BE
RESTORED AGAIN

Any discussion of whether Christians can fall away and lose their salvation will sooner or later turn to a treatment of Hebrews 6. Because this text is so central to discussions about perseverance, we will take a close look at it. Hebrews 6:1–6 reads as follows:

> Therefore let us leave the elementary doctrine of Christ and go on to maturity, not laying again a foundation of repentance from dead works and

of faith toward God, and of instruction about washings, the laying on of hands, the resurrection of the dead, and eternal judgment. And this we will do if God permits. For it is impossible, in the case of those who have once been enlightened, who have tasted the heavenly gift, and have shared in the Holy Spirit, and have tasted the goodness of the word of God and the powers of the age to come, and then have fallen away, to restore them again to repentance, since they are crucifying once again the Son of God to their own harm and holding him up to contempt.

This text not only speaks of those who fall away, but it also gives a vivid description of the state of these people before they fall away. We're also told in this text that it is impossible for these people to be restored again to repentance. If there's any passage in the Bible that speaks about an unpardonable offense, then it is in this strong admonition in Hebrews 6.

This is an extremely difficult passage to interpret. Part of the difficulty has to do with the lack of background information, including the identity of the author of the book of

Hebrews, that would help us understand this teaching in context. Sometimes knowing the author of a certain work gives us clues to understanding difficult passages that come from their pen.

More important, however, is knowing the occasion that provoked this warning in the first place. We know that the author is concerned about a very serious error that was enticing his readers, but we're not sure exactly what that error was. There have been several alternatives suggested by biblical interpreters.

One of the most frequent suggestions is that the author is writing to people who are facing radical persecution and who are in danger of denying Christ in the face of such persecution. He says that in their struggle against sin, his readers "have not yet resisted to the point of shedding [their] blood" (12:4).

In the early church, one of the most rigorous disputes was called the Novatianist Controversy, which arose in the wake of a round of persecution under the Emperor Decius in AD 250. After the persecution ended, church leaders faced the question of what to do with the *lapsi*—those who had renounced the faith under duress, but who now wanted to be readmitted to the church. Many opposed their restoration, including the followers of Novatian, a pretender to the bishopric at Rome. You can understand the passion that people would have in a situation like that. If your father, for example, had kept the faith and was burned at the stake while the next-door neighbor denied the faith and escaped that kind of torment, and then your neighbor wanted to come back into the fellowship of the church after the persecution ended, it is understandable that the martyr's family would have a hard time dealing with that person. The church at large, however, moved for leniency and forgiveness and opted to restore the *lapsi*. So, one possibility is that this passage is speaking of those who fall away from the visible church in the face of persecution but then want to associate with the visible church again in a time of tranquility.

Another frequent suggestion regarding these statements in Hebrews pertains to one of the most virulent heresies to attack the first-century church, the Judaizing heresy. Followers of this view taught that the new covenant community had to continue the practice of observing Old Testament practices, especially circumcision. This heresy is dealt with again and again in the New Testament, most emphatically in the book of Galatians. Some imagine that this passage prohibits Christians from returning to Jewish practices and makes the argument that to do so is to reject the value of Christ's death and resurrection.

Let's look again at what is said in this passage about those who cannot be restored. They are described in these terms: "those who have once been enlightened, who have tasted the heavenly gift, and have shared in the Holy Spirit, and have tasted the goodness of the word of God and the powers of the age to come" (vv. 4–5). What kind of person can be described in these terms? On the surface, it certainly sounds as if the author is describing a Christian, a regenerate person, one who has been spiritually reborn. If that's the case, then the author is saying that it would be impossible for a truly converted person to be restored again to salvation if he has committed the sin that is in view here.

However, this language doesn't necessarily have to be referring to one who is authentically converted. It could refer to people who have been closely involved in the life of the church but were never converted in the first place. As was Old Testament Israel, the New Testament church is what Augustine called a *corpus permixtum*, a mixed body, containing within it what Jesus described as the wheat and the tares (Matt. 13:24–30)—believers and unbelievers.

The tares are those who never were converted, even though they are members of the covenant community.

The Bible describes three groups of people with respect to the church, the visible covenant community. Outside the church, there are unbelievers; inside the church, there are believers (those who have been truly converted) and there are also some unbelievers. Can we say of members of this third group—unbelievers inside the church—that they have been enlightened? Yes, to the extent that they have heard the gospel; they have heard the preaching of the Word. They are not in some remote area where special revelation has never penetrated. They've had the benefit of light when it comes to hearing the Word of God. To say that someone has been enlightened is not necessarily to say that they have been converted.

What about the next description: they've tasted the heavenly gift? It's possible that the gift here is available not only to the converted, but to the unconverted as well. For instance, the gift may be something akin to the manna that God provided for the people of Israel in the wilderness. The Israelites tasted of a heavenly gift, yet some of them remained unconverted. Likewise, looking at a New Testament practice, unbelievers in the church still come to the

Lord's Table. They literally taste the heavenly gift, yet they are still unconverted. A heavenly gift can be given to both believers and unbelievers.

What about sharing in the Holy Spirit? That sounds a little bit more difficult, because we think of sharing in the Holy Spirit as being an experience that only comes to those who have been regenerated and filled by the Holy Spirit. Such an interpretation would be the prima facie reading of that text. But in a broader sense, anyone who's in the middle of the life of the church in a loose sense partakes of the benefits of the power and the presence of the Holy Spirit, because the Spirit dwells and works in the church. Such a person has not necessarily received one specific work of the Holy Spirit—namely, regeneration—but has tasted the good Word of God.

Returning to the overall meaning of this passage, some understand it as referring to people inside the church who are truly converted but who apostatize and repudiate the gospel under persecution; these people, then, cannot be restored. Others see it as referring to the Judaizing heresy. An interpretation that understands the passage as referring to the Judaizing heresy is more likely, because there are a couple of problems with the first view. The first problem is that Peter repudiated the gospel in one sense when he sided with the Judaizers—in that his behavior denied the sufficiency of the work of Christ for salvation (Gal. 2:11–14)—but he was restored. He also denied Christ but was restored by Jesus Himself. So, Peter is an example of one who was restored after repudiating the gospel. This seems to illustrate that the passage must mean something else.

Second, the author of Hebrews says "it is impossible . . . to restore them again to repentance" (vv. 4, 6). The word "again" strongly indicates that there had been at least one previous repentance. If we understand repentance as referring in the New Testament to something that is provoked by the work of the Holy Spirit within us, not just outside of us, and if we are Reformed in our theology and see repentance as a fruit of regeneration and not the cause of regeneration, then we have the tightest difficulty here. Because those who are Reformed in their theology have to say that if a person who genuinely repents is regenerate, a true believer.

Of course, one could argue that there is such a thing as a false repentance—the author of Hebrews mentions Esau as an example (12:16–17). And one who has repented falsely once could do so again. But in that case, the author would not speak of being restored *again* unto repentance, because the first repentance was false. It must be that the author is referring to true repentance, and he is saying that it is impossible for a truly regenerate person, one who has truly repented, to be restored again to repentance if he falls away, because in his falling away he crucifies again the Son of God and holds Him up to contempt. The author is saying that if you do this, you're finished. There is no possibility of restoration if you fall away to this degree.

The argument here is a form of argumentation found throughout the New Testament epistles called the *argumentum ad absurdum*. This means that you take the premises of your opponent and show how, if they are true, they eventually lead to a conclusion that is absurd. Therefore, the premises are to be rejected. Paul uses this argument in 1 Corinthians 15 when speaking of the resurrection of Christ.

When it comes to the Judaizing heresy, the issue turns on the keeping of the law. If the Christian who has embraced the gospel of justification by faith alone now turns back to trying to justify himself through the works of the law—circumcision, keeping the festivals, observing the food laws, etc.—that person cannot be saved, because he has crucified Christ anew.

But what does it mean to crucify Christ anew? Christ obviously has only been crucified once. When He was crucified, Christ took upon Himself the curse of the old covenant. When a person turns back to keeping the law as the primary mode of relating to God, he rejects the work of Christ, who took on the curse on behalf of others. Having repudiated the work of Christ as a vicarious sacrifice, he in fact condemns Christ as been justifiably killed on the cross and makes himself complicit in the death of Christ. Such a person takes the curse upon himself again and cannot be saved.

Thus, we see how the author of Hebrews uses the *argumentum ad absurdum* to demonstrate the folly of his opponents' position. Since the Judaizers' argument that the law should still be observed leads to the repudiation of Christ's work and the loss of salvation, their argument should be rejected.

The author is likely using this argument hypothetically, to show what *would* happen. But this could never actually happen in the case of someone who has truly been converted. The author says in v. 9, "Though we speak in this way, yet in your case, beloved, we feel sure of better things—things that belong to salvation." When he says, "we speak in this way," he is saying that he's writing *in a manner of speaking*, that is, for the sake of argument. He's showing how his opponents' teachings would lead to someone's having no grounds for salvation. But, in the case of true believers, he is certain that they will stand fast: "we feel sure of better things—things that belong to salvation." Therefore, rather than taking away our confidence in perseverance, this passage in fact should strengthen it.

The author of Hebrews wraps up this section with an exhortation: "And we desire each one of you to show the same earnestness to have the full assurance of hope until the end, so that you may not be sluggish, but imitators of those who through faith and patience inherit the promises" (vv. 11–12). This is a call to diligence. The author is reminding his readers that even though they have a hope for the future that they can rest in, the hope that God has given them of the certainty of their salvation should not lead them to sluggishness in living out their faith. The doctrine of eternal security should not lead us to take it easy and stop pressing into the kingdom of God; it should, rather, lead us to live out our faith with greater confidence and zeal.

Chapter Five

THE GIFT OF
PERSEVERANCE

The concept of the perseverance of the saints can be easily misunderstood. In our everyday speech, we talk about persevering as something that we accomplish chiefly through our own concerted efforts. And though the New Testament calls us to persevere—it frequently uses the word *endure*, as in "the one who endures to the end will be saved" (Matt. 24:13)—placing the accent on persevering can cause us to miss the chief truth that supports this concept.

The first theologian to offer an extensive explanation

of the doctrine of perseverance was Augustine of Hippo. The Latin phrase that he used was *donum perseverantiae*, meaning "the gift of perseverance." By this phrase, Augustine meant that perseverance in the life of the Christian is not an achievement accomplished solely by human effort, but a gift. Augustine taught that the only way anyone ever perseveres to the end after beginning the Christian life is by virtue of the grace of God. Since that time, perseverance has been understood as a gift of divine grace.

That's why, when discussing the perseverance of the saints, many English-speaking theologians have found it preferable to speak of the *preservation* of the saints—that is, God *preserves* His own. If I look to myself, I can have no confidence in my ability to continue on to glory once I begin my Christian walk because, as we have noted, the Christian life is a struggle. Paul articulated this in terms of spiritual warfare: the beginning of the Christian life involves liberation from the bondage to the flesh, and we are indwelt by God the Holy Spirit; once we become Christians, we embark upon a whole new life in which we're engaged in the pursuit of our sanctification (Rom. 6:17–19). But that life, as Paul said, is marked by an ongoing battle between the new man and the old man, between the spiritual self and the sinful flesh that still retains power in our lives (7:13–25). But now we have something added as a gift, namely, the presence and power of the Holy Spirit.

Paul calls the Philippian believers to "work out your own salvation with fear and trembling" (Phil. 2:12). In using this phrase, Paul does not mean to say that we earn our salvation by means of our works, but that our obedience (see his commendation of his readers' obedience earlier in the verse) plays a role in our sanctification. In turn, our sanctification plays a role in our persevering.

This is a clear call to labor, to toil, to put forth effort, and this effort is not to be casual, light-hearted, or cavalier. The phrase "fear and trembling" calls attention to the sobriety and earnestness with which we are called to press into the kingdom of God. Jonathan Edwards once said in a sermon that seeking the kingdom of God should be the urgent, primary business of the Christian. We are called to work as hard as we can to persevere.

Note what follows this exhortation: "For it is God who works in you, both to will and to work for his good pleasure" (v. 13). Here we see an example of the New Testament's description of the Christian struggle for perseverance as a *synergistic* work. *Synergism* refers to a work that is done by two or more people. By contrast, *monergism* means that only one person is exercising power or effort.

These words have a checkered background within the history of theology because Reformed scholars and pastors have insisted over and over again that the first step in our salvation is a monergistic work of God. That is, Reformed theologians maintain that the Christian life begins at regeneration, which is the work of the Holy Spirit in quickening us and raising us from a state spiritual death to make us alive in Christ. This is nothing short of a spiritual resurrection, and it is accomplished by God alone, without any human effort. Reformed theologians thus use the word *monergism* or *monergistic* to describe the process of regeneration. As a result, many people who hear this tend to think that a Reformed perspective teaches that the whole Christian life is monergistic.

Have you ever heard the phrase "Let go and let God"? In one sense, that's a perfectly good phrase, because sometimes we rely on ourselves so much that we fail to find rest in God. But the phrase can become a kind of license for what we call "quietism." This is a view that says, "If God wants to change me and if God wants me to grow spiritually, it's His job to do it, and I'm only as strong spiritually as God makes me." A person who thinks this way rewrites the apostolic admonition: "It is God who works in me, both to will and to work—so I don't have to work out my salvation with fear and trembling."

This is a distortion—the passage calls us to labor because God is working *in* us and *with* us; thus, the whole process of persevering is a *synergistic* action, not a *monergistic* one. I am called to work, and God is working as well. In the final analysis, whether my labor becomes fruitful depends on the *donum perseverantiae*, that is, on the gift of perseverance on God's part to preserve me to the end.

Let's look for a moment at Paul's teaching in his letter to the Philippians:

> I thank my God in all my remembrance of you, always in every prayer of mine for you all making my prayer with joy, because of your partnership in the gospel from the first day until now. And I am sure of this, that he who began a good work in you will bring it to completion at the day of Jesus Christ. (Phil. 1:3–6)

Here, Paul speaks of confidence, saying he is "sure of this." What is it that provokes this confidence in the Apostle Paul? He doesn't leave it unnamed. He goes on to say that "he who began a good work in you will bring it to completion at the day of Jesus Christ." Therein lies our confidence and our security: the God who has initiated a person's salvation is not going to allow that redemptive work to be an exercise in futility. God finishes what He starts in His redemptive work in us by preserving those whom He redeems. That's where Paul gains his confidence, and I think that should also be the primary basis for *our* confidence.

Paul fleshes out this basis for our confidence in his letter to the Ephesians. He says, "In him you also, when you heard the word of truth, the gospel of your salvation, and believed in him, were sealed with the promised Holy Spirit, who is the guarantee of our inheritance until we acquire possession of it, to the praise of his glory" (Eph. 1:13). The word translated "sealed" referred in the ancient world to the practice of kings in using signet rings to certify documents. The king had a particular insignia on his ring and would press his ring into a wax seal, leaving a permanent impression on the document, which would indicate the promise and guarantee of the royal decree. Paul uses the word here to say that God seals every Christian by the word of His promise so that our confidence rests not in our own striving, but in the promise of our future redemption, a promise made to us by God. He seals this promise by giving us the Holy Spirit, who is the present, personal indwelling certification of the fullness of redemption that God has wrought within each believer.

Paul says the Holy Spirit "is the guarantee of our inheritance until we acquire possession of it, to the praise of his glory" (v. 14). The word translated "guarantee" is sometimes rendered "earnest." When a person is buying a home, in certain states he may be required to put down a nonrefundable deposit that is called "earnest money." This deposit is the buyer's guarantee that he is going to make the final payment and finish the transaction; it shows that he is "earnest" or "serious" about seeing the process through. Paul uses this commercial language to say that the Holy Spirit is the "earnest" or "guarantee" that we will finally and fully be redeemed. And when the Spirit of truth makes a pledge for a future promise, it is absolutely guaranteed. That promise cannot be broken.

One of the most beloved verses in the Bible is Romans

8:28, which gives us a precious promise from God: "And we know that for those who love God all things work together for good, for those who are called according to his purpose." This is followed by what is often called the "Golden Chain of salvation": "For those whom he foreknew he also predestined to be conformed to the image of his Son, in order that he might be the firstborn among many brothers. And those whom he predestined he also called, and those whom he called he also justified, and those whom he justified he also glorified" (vv. 29–30). This passage is an *elliptical* statement; it assumes a word that is omitted but understood in context. In this case, the assumed word is *all*. *All* those who are predestined are called, not just some of them; *all* who are called are justified; and *all* who are justified are glorified. To be glorified means to enter into the full and final consummation of our salvation. It is from promises such as these that we gain our confidence in God's gift of perseverance.

Chapter Six

THE CARNAL
CHRISTIAN

I used to teach the staff and volunteers of a prominent youth ministry. In those days, these young evangelists would sometimes use a peculiar expression, one not found in the pages of learned tomes of systematic theology: "tube it." The first time I heard it was when one staff member came up and asked me, "Dr. Sproul, why is it that so many of our kids tube it?" I didn't know what he meant—rafting trips down the river? But he explained that they would often have young people who would be introduced to the ministry, begin enthusiastically attending their programs, make a profession of faith in Christ, and then, after a while, would "tube it," meaning their faith would go down the tubes.

People can stand up and make a profession of faith or walk down an aisle at an evangelistic meeting for all kinds of reasons apart from having been genuinely converted. We don't have the ability to read people's hearts. We don't know whether their professions of faith are sincere and genuine. We work on the basis of the outward manifestations and evidences, but we don't know for sure what's going on inside their hearts.

Just look at Judas. He was part of Jesus' inner circle and an eyewitness of some of the most marvelous acts that were ever performed by Jesus. He went to Jesus' "seminary." He sat in His classes every day for three years. He was entrusted as the treasurer of the organization. But Judas tubed it. Actually, to say that Judas tubed it would be a monumental understatement. And yet, Jesus speaks about Judas as one who was actually the son of perdition, one who was really unconverted from the beginning (John 17:12). Judas' profession of faith was spurious. It was not authentic.

This is not just a problem for evangelistic or youth

ministries. It's a problem in the life of the church as a whole. As a result, we need to be careful about what we say—while we can affirm that someone has made a profession of faith, we are unable to confirm whether that person has been truly converted.

A related development is the emergence of an innovative doctrine in popular Christianity: the idea of the "carnal Christian." Historically, this idea was linked to the theology of dispensationalism. It erupted in the 1980s into the Lordship Salvation Controversy, an intramural debate among dispensationalists. One side insisted that it is faith alone—not faith plus repentance—that saves; therefore, it is possible to receive Christ as Savior but not as Lord. The other side argued that faith and repentance are two sides of the same coin.

Both sides agreed that everyone who comes to faith *should* put their trust in Christ as both Savior and Lord, and every believer *should* bring forth the fruit of conversion and works of obedience to Christ. The issue turned on whether it is possible to be saved without embracing Christ as Lord and therefore exhibiting works of obedience. The one who is saved without embracing Christ as Lord is one we might call a "carnal Christian."

The controversy resulted in a distinction among different types of Christians. These types are illustrated in a popular evangelistic tract used for many years by Cru (formerly Campus Crusade for Christ). The three distinct types are defined graphically in terms of three circles displayed in a row, with each circle representing a particular type of person. At the center of each circle is a silhouette of a chair, which represents the throne of a person's life, the seat of authority.

In the first circle, to the far left, on the chair is the letter *S*, which stands for "self." This signifies the egocentricity of the unconverted person. This is the person who has not received Christ, who has not submitted to Christ in any way. And outside the circle is the figure of the cross, which means that in this person's life, self—what we would call "the flesh"—dominates. The fallen human nature is in control, and Christ is not in that person's life.

The third circle, to the far right, has Christ, the cross, on the throne. This is the Spirit-filled life. Jesus Christ is the central authority in the life of this person. This represents the mature Christian who has grown up to embrace Christ not only as Savior but also as Lord.

The middle circle portrays a strange little picture. There is the chair in the middle, with the *S* for "self," but below the chair is the cross. This image represents a person who has Christ in his life, but He has not ascended to the throne. The self is still on the throne; the flesh still rules. Hence, this person is described as the carnal Christian. The carnal Christian is a person who is a Christian but whose Christian life is still dominated by carnality.

Where does this idea come from biblically? The biblical justification for this is that the New Testament does speak about carnal Christians. In 1 Corinthians 3, the Apostle Paul is rebuking the Corinthian Christians, and he says:

> But I, brothers, could not address you as spiritual people, but as people of the flesh, as infants in Christ. I fed you with milk, not solid food, for you were not ready for it. And even now you are not yet ready, for you are still of the flesh. For while there is jealousy and strife among you, are you not of the flesh and behaving only in a human way? For when one says, "I follow Paul," and another, "I follow Apollos," are you not being merely human? (1 Cor. 3:1–4)

Paul is clearly talking about people whom he regards as believers. He calls them "brothers," and yet he also describes them as being "of the flesh," that is, carnal. So, what's wrong with the idea of talking about "carnal Christians"? Not only does Paul describe the Corinthian believers as carnal in this case, but he also refers to himself as "of the flesh" in Romans 7 when he is talking about his own struggles in sanctification: "I am of the flesh, sold under sin" (v. 14). All of this seems to suggest that "carnal Christian" might be a useful, and biblically sound, way of talking about a certain kind of Christian.

The descriptor "carnal" or "fleshly" also recurs in the New Testament. Earlier, we saw that Paul speaks of the struggle of the Christian life as warfare between the flesh and the spirit. And we also know that that same metaphor of *flesh* is used repeatedly in the New Testament to describe the condition of the unbeliever. The unbeliever is pure flesh. That's why Jesus says you have to be born again in order to see the kingdom of God, because what is born of the flesh is flesh, and we are by nature fleshly or fallen. The unregenerate person is not engaged in warfare between the spirit in the flesh; he is totally in the flesh, totally carnal.

Based on these distinctions, we might assume that in the

image from the booklet, the idea is not that the person is still purely in the flesh, because Christ is in his life. Rather, it is meant to communicate that there are three kinds of people: unbelievers, baby believers, and mature believers. That's a perfectly legitimate distinction, because that's what Paul is doing in 1 Corinthians 3 when he calls the Corinthian Christians "of the flesh." He's calling them "of the flesh" because they are still babies and because their behavior is showing more of the ongoing manifestation of the flesh than of the maturity that comes from the fruit of the Spirit.

But the idea in the New Testament is that no person in this life is totally spiritual and no Christian in this world is totally carnal. So when we speak of carnal Christians, if by that term we mean baby Christians, everything is well and good. But if we mean people who have received Christ as their Savior but not as their Lord, where the self still dominates and rules the life, who are we describing? We're describing the unconverted person, the person who's in the church and around the fellowship of Christ, the person who is professing Jesus Christ, but is really not a Christian at all. The idea of a carnal Christian in the sense of one who is totally carnal is an oxymoron. There is no totally carnal Christian, just as there is no totally spiritual Christian.

I wish I could point to an easy way to move from infancy in the faith to adulthood. The Apostle Paul speaks of our need to be nourished and nurtured. He also uses the image of babies as requiring a milk diet because they aren't yet ready to eat solid food.

It takes time to reach spiritual maturity. But what's scary is when we hear of people who have been in the faith for ten years or fifteen years and they're still drinking milk. That was what was distressing the Apostle here in his letter to the Corinthians. The time for their infancy was long past, and he was calling them now to a solid diet of the things of God, to chewing on the meat of the gospel, which is part of the whole life of persevering in Christ.

Chapter Seven

OUR GREAT
HIGH PRIEST

Many of us have taken comfort in the intercessory prayer of a friend or a pastor. How much more comfort, then, can we experience from the full assurance that Jesus is praying for us? Have you ever had people ask you, "Pray for me," and you say, "Sure, I'll pray for you," and then you forget? I know that in my lifetime, I have told people that I would pray for them and I forget. If I remember at some point later, I will stop and pray, but often it's only out of guilt—so that if that person asks whether I prayed, I can tell them that I did.

Intercessory prayer is comforting, but we humans can't always be relied on to follow through with our promises to pray. This is not so with Christ. The New Testament speaks of Him as our Great High Priest. As our Great High Priest, He has offered up the perfect sacrifice—Himself—but His priestly work did not end on the cross. Every day, in the presence of the Father, Christ intercedes for His people (Heb. 7:25). "The prayer of a righteous person has great power as it is working," James tells us (5:16), but no prayer has the same power as the prayers of Christ.

The intercession of our Great High Priest is the foundation for our confidence when it comes to our perseverance. It also helps us make sense of the accounts of Peter and Judas, two of Jesus' disciples who experienced a serious fall. One disciple's fall away from Christ is seen as a final and full work of apostasy, whereas the other disciple's fall is not final and full because he is restored. And we see that their crime against Christ was very similar. Judas betrayed Jesus. And that same night, Peter denied Christ.

These two men who had been disciples with Jesus during his earthly ministry committed treason against Him in his darkest hour. And there are further similarities in these two examples in that Jesus predicted both Peter's and Judas' diabolical acts. But we recall that when Jesus said, "One of you will betray me," the disciples said among themselves, "Who is it, Lord? Is it I?" When Judas asked, "Is it I, Rabbi?" Jesus said to him, "You have said so" (Matt. 26:25). Jesus' final words to Judas were "What you are going to do, do quickly" (John 13:27). And He dismissed him from their presence.

When Jesus prophesied that Peter would deny him, Peter protested profusely. "Though they all fall away because of you, I will never fall away," he said (Matt. 26:33). This brings to mind Paul's admonition, "Let anyone who thinks that he stands take heed lest he fall" (1 Cor. 10:12), because Jesus then turned to Simon and said to him in loving terms, "Simon, Simon, behold, Satan demanded to have you, that he might sift you like wheat" (Luke 22:31).

Sifting wheat is not a laborious task that only the strong can perform. It may take time and it may be tedious, but it's not labor intensive. In using this metaphor, Jesus is cautioning Simon not to rely on his own strength, because it would be an easy thing for Satan to entice him to fall. Satan is stronger than Peter, and would have no trouble overcoming whatever strength Peter thought he had.

Notice, however, that Jesus does not say to Peter, "What

you are going to do, do quickly." Our Lord's words to Simon Peter were significantly different from what He said to Judas. He said, "I have prayed for you that your faith may not fail. And when you have turned again, strengthen your brothers" (Luke 22:32).

Notice what Jesus doesn't say. He doesn't simply *hope* that Peter will be able to resist Satan, or that he will return, or that he will be able to strengthen the brothers. He expresses certainty that Peter *will* do these things. There was no doubt in Jesus' mind not only that Peter would fall, and fall abysmally, but also that Peter would be restored. Indeed, history testifies that Peter, in spite of this radical and serious fall, nevertheless endured to the end. He repented, he was forgiven, he was restored, and he endured to the end.

The rest of the teaching of the New Testament hints at a causal connection between the words "I have prayed for you" and "when you turn." Jesus is our Great High Priest who, upon His ascension, sat down at the right hand of God. There, He lives to make intercession for His people.

Our greatest consolation when it comes to our eternal security comes from the full assurance of the present work of Christ on our behalf. When Jesus died on the cross, He cried out, "It is finished" (John 19:30). His atoning death purchased redemption for His people, but Christ's redemptive work didn't end on the cross. After His death, He was raised for our justification. Then He ascended into heaven, where He sat down at the right hand of God. There He rules as the King of kings and the Lord of lords, governing the universe and ruling over His church. All this comes under the heading of the finished work of Christ.

We get a glimpse of Christ's intercession for us in the Upper Room Discourse in John 13–17, and especially the High Priestly Prayer in chapter 17. In this discourse, Jesus instructs and comforts His disciples. As they are approaching their darkest hour, Jesus offers security to combat their anxiety, saying:

Let not your hearts be troubled. Believe in God; believe also in me. In my Father's house are many rooms. If it were not so, would I have told you that I go to prepare a place for you? And if I go and prepare a place for you, I will come again and will take you to myself, that where I am you may be also. (John 14:1–3)

When the Lord says He will go and prepare a place for the disciples, He's talking about something that He is going to do not in that very moment, but at a certain point in the future. Instead of talking to them about the cross, He looks beyond it, to His ascension, where He would enter into the heavenly tabernacle in order to prepare a place for His people. And later, He will return again to gather His people. The New Testament often speaks of the consummation of the redemption of the bride of Christ, the true people of God, in terms of a final glorious reunion between Christ and His people.

Later on in this same discourse, we read Christ's High Priestly Prayer:

> When Jesus had spoken these words, he lifted up his eyes to heaven, and said, "Father, the hour has come; glorify your Son that the Son may glorify you, since you have given him authority over all flesh, to give eternal life to all whom you have given him. And this is eternal life, that they know you the only true God, and Jesus Christ whom you have sent. I glorified you on earth, having accomplished the work that you gave me to do.

And now, Father, glorify me in your own presence with the glory that I had with you before the world existed.

I have manifested your name to the people whom you gave me out of the world. Yours they were, and you gave them to me, and they have kept your word. Now they know that everything that you have given me is from you. For I have given them the words that you gave me, and they have received them and have come to know in truth that I came from you; and they have believed that you sent me. I am praying for them. I am not praying for the world but for those whom you have given me, for they are yours. All mine are yours, and yours are mine, and I am glorified in them. And I am no longer in the world, but they are in the world, and I am coming to you. Holy Father, keep them in your name, which you have given me, that they may be one, even as we are one. While I was with them, I kept them in your name, which you have given me. I have guarded them, and not one of them has been lost except the son of destruction, that the Scripture might be fulfilled. . . . I do not ask for these only, but also for those who will believe in me through their word, that they may all be one, just as you, Father, are in me, and I in you, that they also may be in us, so that the world may believe that you have sent me. (John 17:1–12, 20–21)

Jesus begins by recalling the covenant within the Godhead itself to save some, the elect, from among the mass of humanity. He asks that the Father would glorify Him upon the completion of His work. He then goes on to pray for the disciples, and not for the disciples only, but also for "those who will believe in me through their word" (v. 20), which includes us.

Jesus acknowledges that one was lost, but as the Scripture elsewhere declares, it was the one who was the son of perdition from the beginning. Judas' fall was final. He was a true apostate, one who made a profession of faith though he was never really converted. He was the son of perdition from the beginning. Peter, on the other hand, was not lost. He turned again and was restored. Christ's intercessory prayers upheld him.

The whole point of Jesus' prayer is that none whom the

Father has given to the Son are lost. No one, He said, can snatch them out of His hand (John 10:28). We persevere because we are preserved, and we are preserved because of the intercession of our Great High Priest. This is our greatest consolation and our greatest source of confidence that we will persevere in the Christian life.

Further your Bible study with *Tabletalk* magazine, another learning tool from R.C. Sproul.

....

TABLETALK MAGAZINE FEATURES:

- A Bible study for each day—bringing the best in biblical scholarship together with down-to-earth writing, *Tabletalk* helps you understand the Bible and apply it to daily living.

- Trusted theological resource—*Tabletalk* avoids trends, shallow doctrine and popular movements to present biblical truth simply and clearly.

- Thought-provoking topics—each issue contains challenging, stimulating articles on a wide variety of topics related to theology and Christian living.

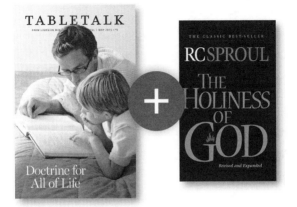

Sign up for a free 3-month trial of *Tabletalk* magazine and we will send you R.C. Sproul's *The Holiness of God*

TryTabletalk.com/CQ

About the Author

Dr. R.C. Sproul is the founder and chairman of Ligonier Ministries, an international Christian discipleship organization located near Orlando, Fla. He also serves as copastor at Saint Andrew's Chapel in Sanford, Fla., as chancellor of Reformation Bible College, and as executive editor of *Tabletalk* magazine. His teaching can be heard around the world on the daily radio program *Renewing Your Mind*.

During his distinguished academic career, Dr. Sproul helped train men for the ministry as a professor at several theological seminaries.

He is author of more than ninety books, including *The Holiness of God*, *Chosen by God*, *The Invisible Hand*, *Faith Alone*, *Everyone's a Theologian*, *Truths We Confess*, *The Truth of the Cross*, and *The Prayer of the Lord*. He also served as general editor of the *Reformation Study Bible* and has written several children's books, including *The Donkey Who Carried a King*. Dr. Sproul and his wife, Vesta, make their home in Sanford, Fla.